For Mary Ann

ISBN 13: 978-1-63489-554-5

Library of Congress Catalog Number has been applied for.
Printed in China
First Printing: 2022

26 25 24 23 22   5 4 3 2 1

Cover and interior design by Maren Daniels.

Wise Ink Creative Publishing
807 Broadway St NE
Suite 46
Minneapolis, MN 55413

To order, visit marendanielsart.com.

The Elements of Art

Art

(an elementary art teacher's guide to color, shape, texture & more)

Maren Daniels

Why, hello there!
I'm Ms. Daniels,
your friendly art teacher.

Sometimes my students ask me,

And I reply,
"First, an artist feels an urge to create!"

"Then they will decide which Elements of Art to use."

After all, artists must use at least one of these elements to create a work of art.

here they are

LINE

SHAPE

FORM

TEXTURE

VALUE

SPACE

COLOR

now let's dig in

Line

is a continuous mark

Shape

is an enclosed space or area

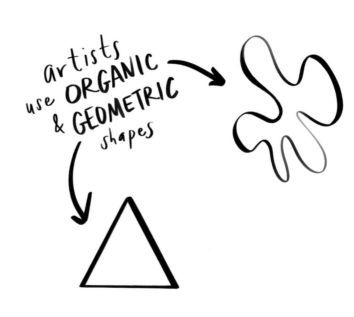

artists use ORGANIC & GEOMETRIC shapes

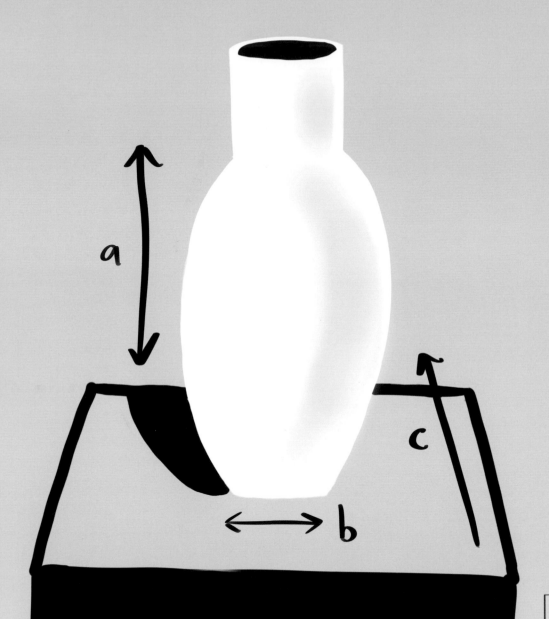

a = height
b = width
c = depth

sculptors, architects, designers, & potters all use FORM

Form

is an object that has three dimensions and takes up space

Texture

is the way something feels
or appears to feel

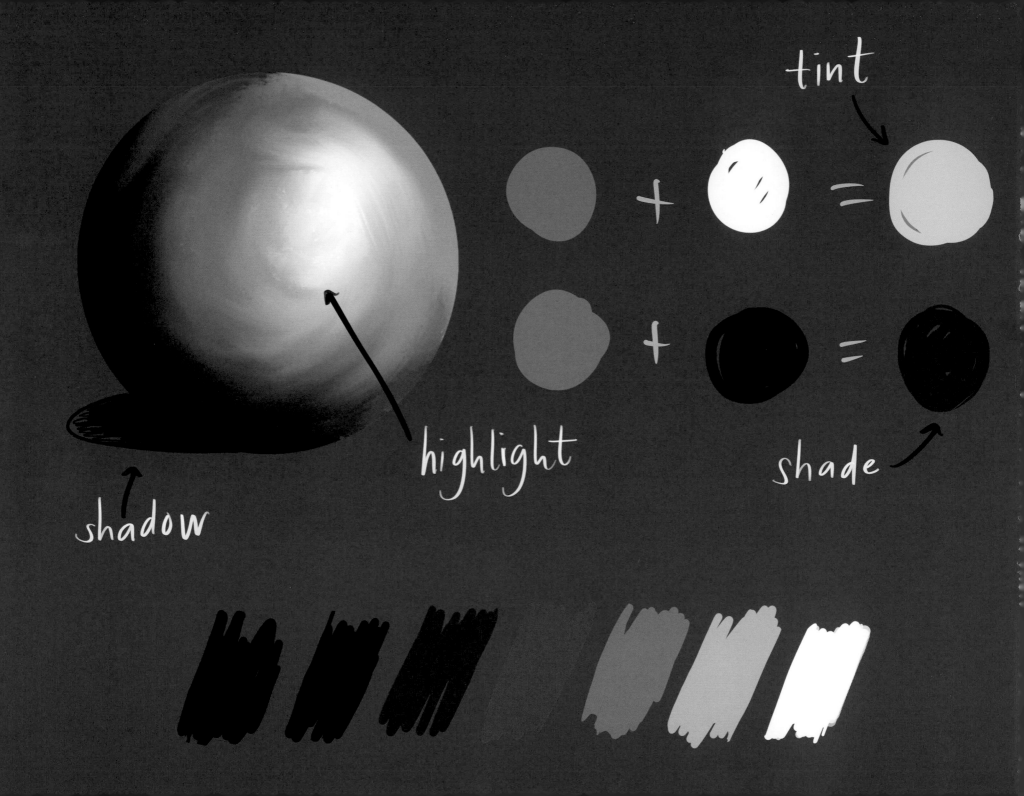

tint

+ =

highlight

shadow

+ = shade

Value

is the lightness or darkness of a color

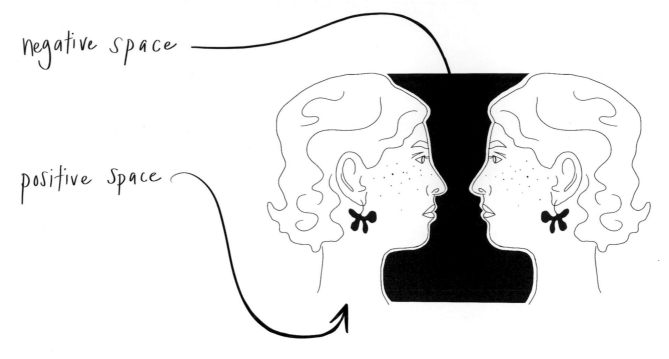

negative space

positive space

Space

is the area around or between images

background

middleground

foreground

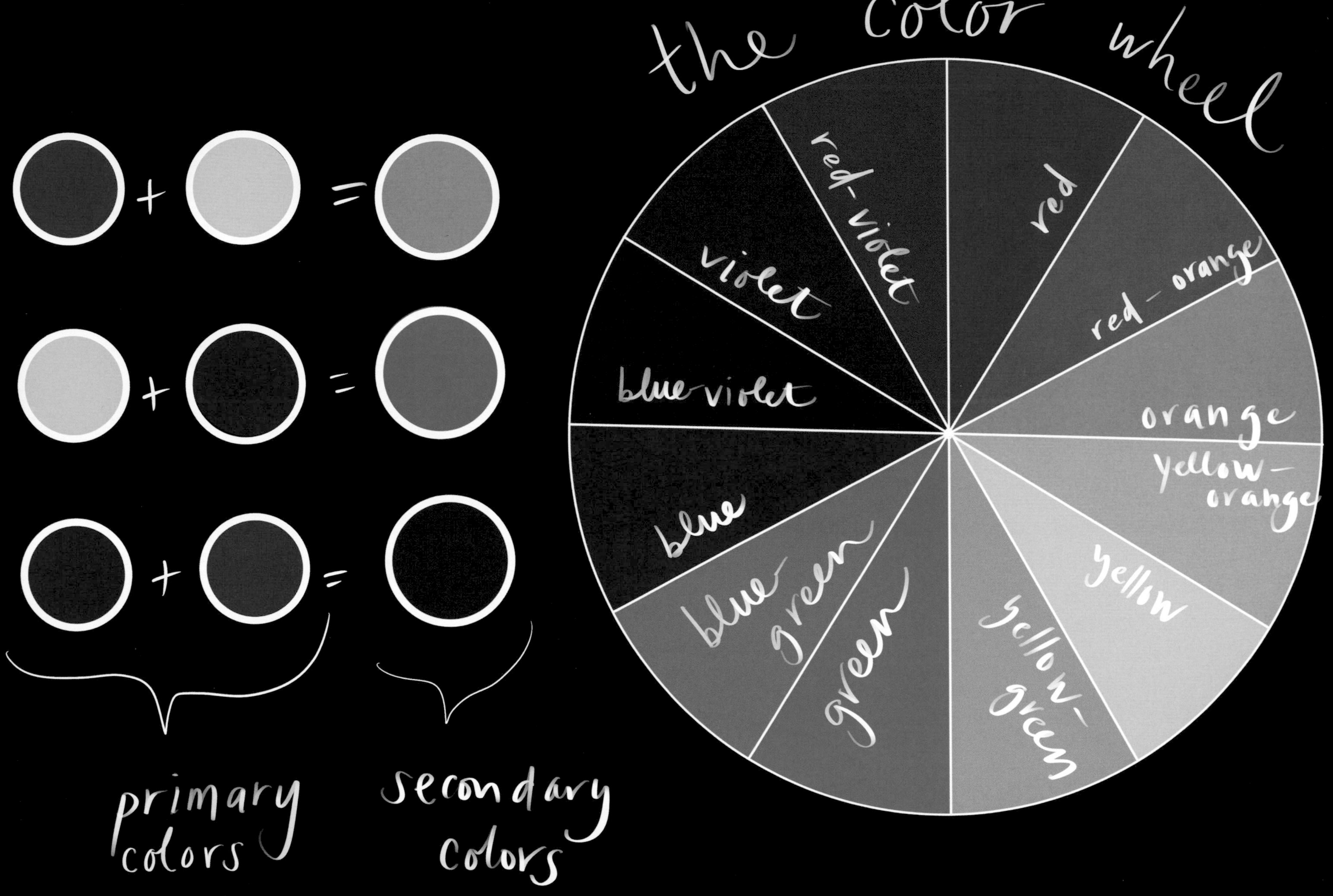

○ + ○ = ○

○ + ○ = ○

○ + ○ = ○

primary colors

secondary colors

the color wheel

red-violet

red

violet

red-orange

blue-violet

orange

yellow-orange

blue

yellow

blue-green

yellow-green

green

Color

red, orange, yellow, green, blue, violet, and many in between

consider which
Elements of Art to use!

your turn
♡ Ms. D.

Activities for future exploration

Beginner

+ Fill a piece of paper with as many different lines as you can. Here are some examples to start you off: wavy, zigzag, spiral, and vertical.

+ Gather various pieces of colored paper. Practice cutting geometric shapes, like triangles, circles, and squares. Then practice cutting organic shapes, like leaves, clouds, or animals. Glue your shapes down to your paper and voilà, you've made a collage.

+ Prepare red, yellow, and blue paint. Get mixing and see what the primary colors can create.

Intermediate

++ Use air-dry clay to create a pinch pot. Start by rolling a ball, stick your thumb in slightly, and repeatedly pinch the sides until it forms a pot.

++ Grab a mirror, paper, and pencil and create a self-portrait. A self-portrait is a picture of yourself. What kinds of shapes can you see in your face?

++ Practice making value by changing the pressure in your drawing tool. Pushing down hard onto your paper will create dark values, and pressing lightly will create light values.

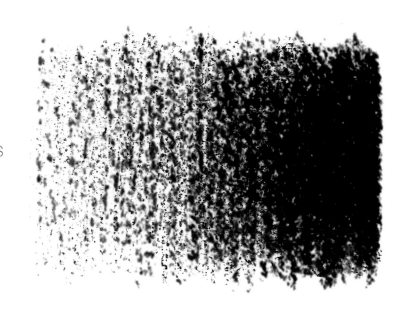

Advanced

+++ Set up your own still life with three to five objects you care about. First, draw the shapes closest to you in the foreground, and continue drawing the objects in the middle ground or background. Overlapping and playing with the size of objects can create an illusion of space.

+++ Build a sculpture using cardboard, tape, yarn, paper, wood, or fabric.

+++ Create a work of art with real and implied textures. Real texture is something you can feel with your hands. You could incorporate yarn or fabric into your piece. Implied texture is when an artist creates an illusion of real texture. You could use thick, rough brushstrokes of paint on a smooth canvas to look like rocky mountains.

Maren Daniels is a public school art teacher in South St. Paul, MN. She lives in Minneapolis with her family. Her favorite Elements of Art to use are line, shape, and color.